ONCE UPON A STRING

Fiddle Fundamentals

by Shamma Sabir

Art and Illustration by Sarah Parsons

Edited by Ronny Schiff

Design and Layout by Charylu Roberts, O.Ruby Productions

Music Typeset by Charylu Roberts and Lily Diamond

Photos by Brett and Kamran Beaulieu

ISBN 978-1-5400-1475-7

EXCLUSIVELY DISTRIBUTED BY

HAL•LEONARD®
7777 W. BLUEMOUND RD. P.O. BOX 13819 MILWAUKEE, WI 53213

Dedication

To my husband, who encourages me to nurture my love of all things music. To my parents, who placed my first fiddle in my hands and encouraged me to grow in music. To all of the teachers along my path who have shared their knowledge and love of music with me. To those I have taught over the years who have inspired me to search for the best, most effective and most compassionate ways to share my learning. A special thanks to Lynda Norman and John McMahon who encouraged me to share my love for teaching music in book form. Finally, thank you to my sisters, Sarah Beaulieu and Roxanna Sabir, as well as my sister in music, Patti Kusturok, for adding your wisdoms to the final product.

About the Author

Photo courtesy of Michael Breakey

Shamma Sabir has been a passionate ambassador of Canadian fiddle music from the time she heard her first notes. From the stage at the Canadian Grand Masters Fiddle Championships to the springy dance floors of Saskatchewan, Shamma has played and taught her way through much of the Canadian landscape.

A devoted teacher, Shamma earned a Masters degree in Clinical Psychology using original research to further her understanding of the dance between music training and brain development. In *Fiddle Fundamentals*, Shamma brings research about learning and the brain, years of experience as a teacher and her love of the power of curiosity and play to culminate in this first book in the *Once Upon A String* series. Shamma can be contacted at *shammasabir.ca*

Credits

Kamran Beaulieu has been making music on his fiddle for two years and he is already a consummate performer. When he's not holding his fiddle, this bright student can be found playing with his collection of tractors.

Sarah Parsons lives in Kelowna, British Columbia. She currently practices her art in Studio 113, The Rotary Centre for the Arts. Sarah's recent painting style involves a love affair with acrylic and mixed media on wood. The beautiful swirling landscapes of the Okanagan Valley are a great inspiration for Sarah's paintings and drawings. Many of her paintings depict animal characters, with a special fondness for pigs. Sarah loves fresh air and quiet moments with nature, enjoying snowshoeing and kayaking. Sarah loves animals, and is a passionate Vegan. Sarah can be contacted at: *sarahparsons.ca*

Brett Beaulieu finds inspiration in the people and the landscapes around him. Brett's photographic lens reflects a passion for children and families in particular, but also a love of the natural world. Brett can often be found out on the trails and waterscapes of the Fraser Valley, looking for the perfect shot. Brett can be contacted at: *kreativeclicksphotography.ca*

Table of Contents

How To Use This Book

*O*NCE UPON A STRING—*Fiddle Fundamentals* is intended for use as a teaching guide for violin or fiddle teachers and as a supplement to lessons. Concepts within each section are delineated in a progressive format in which each step builds upon the previous step. Depending on your level of playing, it may be practical to move through several sections simultaneously. However, within each section I strongly encourage you to move through material in the order in which it is presented.

Left and Right Hand Practice: The object of many of the exercises in this book is to separate left and right hand practice. Trying to tackle technical points on both sides simultaneously can feel overwhelming and defeating. When focusing on *left* hand technique points, do not worry about what your *right* arm may be doing and visa versa. With careful practice, and as you develop automaticity on each side, you will notice that both arms work together to create great tone and intonation.

Warm-Up: It is important to warm up each practice session with bow exercises, scales and easy warm-up pieces. Warm-up exercise and tunes are those that you have already memorized and mastered. Since you no longer need to focus on the bowing and the notes, you can devote your focus towards improving left and right hand technique. *This is a key aspect towards mastery that is often overlooked by students.* Warming up in this way will build and reinforce great technique while making the production of beautiful sound feel more automatic and effortless.

Practice Duration: If you are able to separate your practice into shorter segments, you will find that you progress much faster with intense concentration for a shorter amount of time. I recommend practicing for 10–15 minutes several times a day as opposed to 30–45 minutes one time per day. This is especially true if you are new to the fiddle and have a difficult time maintaining correct posture for longer periods of time.

Body Health: Learning to play the fiddle can lead to soreness in your jaw, neck, shoulders and arms if you are practicing for long periods of time with poor technique. To avoid this, in addition to practicing for shorter periods of time, it is also important to stretch and take breaks in order to notice whether there are any points of tension in your body. It can be very helpful to set a timer in order to help you remember to pause, notice, stretch, and re-orient yourself to healthy technique.

Find a Practice Buddy: The fiddle is an instrument that has traditionally been played at jam sessions and gatherings to add to the festivity of an event. If you can find a group to play with or someone to practice with from time to time, you will enjoy your practice sessions much more!

Practice Checklists: There are many technical aspects to remember as you learn to play the fiddle. In order to help you to focus in on fundamental aspects of playing, I have created *checklists* for you to detach from this book and place on your wall or music stand. It will be helpful to have a visual guide with regard to what you need to remember while you are practicing. Begin by focusing on only one practice point. As it becomes more automatic (i.e., you do not need to make corrections as frequently), add in another practice point until you have mastered the checklists. As you go through your checklists it will be helpful to use a mirror in order to get a good look at your posture and technical setup.

PRACTICE TIP

Whenever you see this symbol, I have given you a tip
that will help you master a certain aspect of your playing.
Pay attention to these sections as they will provide you with helpful
reminders that will help take your playing to the next level!

I CHOOSE A CHALLENGE

This symbol lets you know that if you have mastered the basic
technique and notes in a particular section, you can choose
to try something a little bit more difficult or go a little bit
farther with the concept. Go ahead—challenge yourself!

Parts of the Fiddle

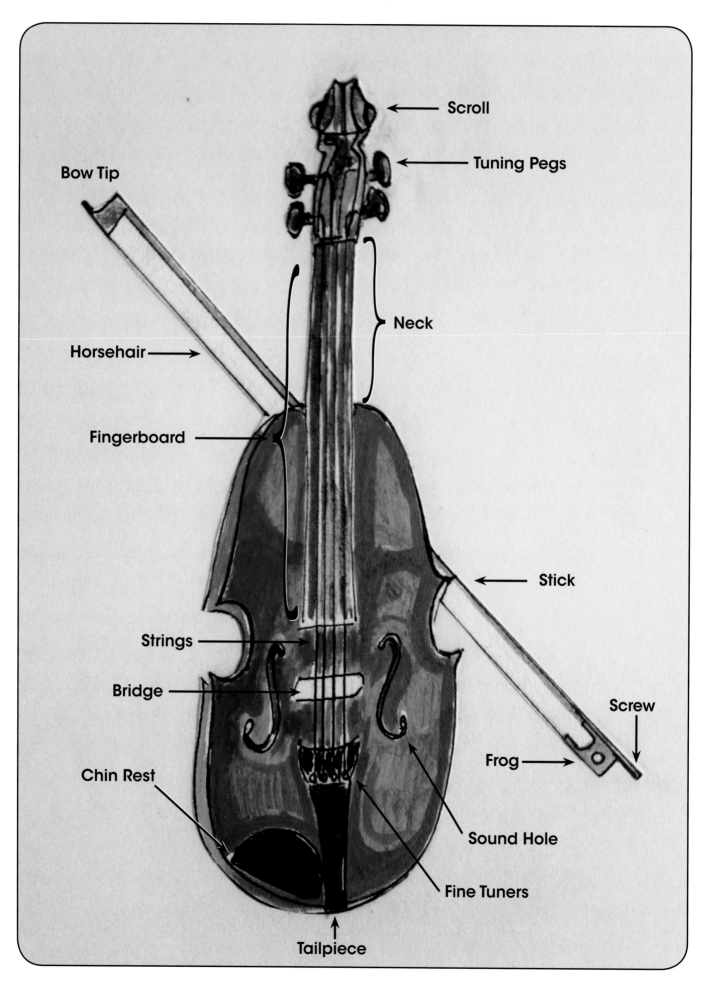

The Bow Hold

How to Hold the Bow

Let me introduce you to the fingers on your right hand—I'll bet you never knew you had such a cool gang of fingers!

1. **Curly:** The pointer finger curls over the grip

2. The **Two Best Friends:** The two middle fingers stick together, just like best friends, and curve around over the frog—kind of like sitting on a bridge and dangling your feet over.

3. **King or Queen of the Castle:** The pinky is nice and round and the tip of the pinky rests on the top of the stick of the bow—it is the only finger that gets to sit right on the stick on the fingertip, so the pinky gets to be the King or Queen of the Castle! For ease of reference, I will just refer to the pinky as the "King of Castle" from here on.

4. **Knuckles the Thumb:** The thumb is nice and round, and leans against the "bump" of the frog. Is your knuckle sticking out? Then you're doing it right!

Are you ready to give it a try? If you're holding the bow correctly, it should look like you are *holding a ball* in the palm of your hand: All of your fingers and the thumb should be rounded.

Now that you've been introduced to your fingers, remember that the *Two Best Friends,* the *King of the Castle, Curly* and *Knuckles* will need checking on often, because they are just learning their new roles! When you're ready, practice checking on them with the two bow exercises on the next page.

Two Easy Bow Hold Exercises

Windshield Wipers

- Begin with the hair of the bow on top, so that you are looking down at your thumb. Check that *Knuckles the Thumb* is bent (knuckle sticking out) and that your fingers are relaxed and curved as well.

- Slowly turn your wrist so that the bow travels from 3 o'clock to 9 o'clock—just like the windshield wipers in your car! As you turn the bow, watch all the fingers on your right hand. *Knuckles the Thumb* should remain bent and the *King of the Castle* (pinky) stays round and on top of the stick of the bow.

- Do a quick check to make sure that *Knuckles the Thumb* is bent, the *Two Best Friends* are still sticking together with their feet over the bridge, the *King of the Castle* is still round and on top of the stick of the bow, and that *Curly* (the pointer finger) is still curled around the grip of the bow.

- When everything is in place, turn the bow slowly back to the 3 o'clock position, and check on your fingers again!

Pinky Push-ups

- Begin by holding the bow horizontally so that the stick is on top and the horse-hair is on the bottom. Make sure that the *King of the Castle* is round and sitting on the stick of the bow, and that *Knuckles the Thumb* is rounded, with the knuckle sticking out;

- Let the *King of the Castle* flex his muscles by slowly pushing down on the bow, keeping it curved as you go. If the *King* is strong, this pressure will bring the tip of the bow up;

- Once you have pressed down as far as you can go while still keeping the *King* rounded, slowly relax the pressure on the *King*, letting the stick of the bow slowly come back down to where you started.

Do this five to ten times before you practice every day, and your fingers will become strong in no time!

PRACTICE TIP

Keep your bow handy: Take your bow out of
the case during your favourite TV show and practice
Windshield Wipers and Pinky Push-ups during commercials.
You will have a perfect bow hold in no time!

I CHOOSE A CHALLENGE

Throughout this book, there will be places where you can
choose a challenge—these challenges will stretch your
knowledge of notes and technique, and are always fun to do!

Here's the first challenge:

The Bow Hold Showdown

For this Challenge, you can race a friend or get someone to
time you to see how fast you are. Sitting down on a chair,
place your bow in your lap. Put your right hand in the air.
As soon as you hear the word "go!", pick up your bow
with your right hand and put your bow hold on as
quickly as possible. The winner is the person who has all of
their fingers in place in the shortest amount of time!

BOW HOLD CHECKLIST

Here's a quick and easy way to double check that everyone is in place and ready to rock! See how fast you can become at going through the short list below to make sure that all of your fingers are in place every time you pick up the bow!

1. Curly: Is the pointer finger curled over the grip?

2. Are the *Two Best Friends* (middle fingers) sticking together, just like best friends, and dangling their feet over the bridge?

3. Is the *King of the Castle* (pinky) nice and round and resting on the top of the stick of the bow?

4. Is *Knuckles the Thumb* also nice and round, leaning against the "bump" of the frog?

The 2 Violin

The Violin

Okay! You're well on your way to mastering the bow hold, and now it's time to create some good habits with the violin. Let's get started!

Holding the Violin

Here are a few steps to follow in order to find the healthiest way to hold the violin, using great technique:

1. First, the violin needs to sit comfortably between your chin and your shoulder. In order to do this properly, you will likely need a good shoulder rest or a sponge.

2. Stand with your back and neck aligned, looking straight ahead. Keep your knees and hips loose and unlocked;

3. With your left foot, take one small step forward and to the left, and center your weight evenly over both feet;

4. Looking up, bring your left shoulder forward slightly as if you were posing for a picture. Place your violin on your shoulder so that when you bring your chin down, it sits comfortably in the chin rest.

5. At this point you should be able to see (if you're using a mirror) that your neck follows in a straight line from your spine. Sometimes I see students lay their cheek in their chin rest like a pillow, but this position can cause strain on your neck and shoulder muscles.

6. Notice where you are looking. If your shoulder rest is too high so that it is forcing you to look up at the ceiling, you need to lower your shoulder rest. If you are looking down, you need to raise your chin rest until your eyes are looking straight across the room. This posture allows you to play without straining your back and neck.

7. CHECK: Your nose, left foot, and the scroll of your violin should all point in the same direction.

checklist ♬

VIOLIN HOLD CHECKLIST

1. Check to make sure your body is *loose* and *relaxed*, and that your hips and knees are not locked;

2. Where are you *looking*? If you are looking up at the ceiling or down at the ground, adjust your shoulder rest so that you are looking straight across the room;

3. Your *left foot* should be slightly forward and to the left so that your weight is evenly balanced over both feet;

4. Your spine and neck should follow in a *straight line* — your chin rest is for resting your chin and part of your jaw, but not your cheek;

5. Your nose, left foot and scroll should all point in the same direction.

Left-Hand Technique

Once you are comfortably set up with the violin under your chin, bring your left hand up to the neck and curve your fingers over the strings.

Some important things about the left hand:

1. Are you serving pizza? Have a look at your left wrist and make sure that it is straight, creating a straight line from your forearm to the back of your hand.

   A common mistake is to flatten the hand against the underside of the neck. If you were to hold your hand out that way in front of you, it would look like you were serving a tray of pizza, so make a choice now to be a fiddler—not a pizza server!

2. When setting your fingers down onto the fingerboard, be sure that you are playing on the tips of your fingers. This will help you to play in tune.

3. Check to make sure that your *thumb is placed opposite to your index finger*, and that the tip of your thumb is just peeking over the top of the fingerboard at your other fingers.

   Imagine that you have drawn a face on your thumb (or you can actually do this!) and only the eyes and eyebrows are peeking over the neck of the violin at the other fingers!

4. *Keep your left hand loose.* In fact, keep your whole body loose! A common challenge for fiddlers is coping with sore muscles, because we often become very tense when we are concentrating hard. Often fiddlers will squeeze the neck of the violin between the thumb and bottom knuckle of the index finger, resulting in a very sore left hand. See the **Practice Tip** below for a great way to stay loose!

PRACTICE TIP

Shake out frequently: Until your body gets used to it, holding the fiddle up for long periods of time can be uncomfortable. For the first few weeks, try setting a timer as a reminder to shake out!

LEFT HAND CHECKLIST

Here's a handy checklist to use so that you know that you are setting up your left hand properly before you use your bow. Keep this list somewhere that's easy to see from your practice space, like on your wall or music stand!

1. *Left Wrist:* Is it nice and straight, or are you serving pizza?

2. Are you playing on the *tips of your fingers?* Check to be sure that your fingers are nice and round.

3. *Thumb and Index Finger Opposite One Another:* Is your thumb "peeking" over the fingerboard at your index finger?

4. Is your left hand nice and *loose?* Be sure to shake out your hands and body as often as you need to!

Using the Bow!
Reel, Waltz and Jig Patterns

Using the Bow!
Reel, Waltz and Jig Patterns

There are three basic types of fiddle tunes that we are going to explore as we learn to play the fiddle—they are *reels, waltzes* and *jigs*. In music notation, the main difference between these three types of tunes is how many beats are in a bar.

These tunes are also types of dances, and because they differ in terms of how many beats are in each bar, they also differ in terms of the steps that the dancers perform to these tunes!

In the old days, especially in the Canadian Prairies and on the East Coast of Canada, people used to get together frequently to sing and dance to fiddle music. There are places in Canada where this still happens, so you never know—you too might play for a good, old-fashioned barn dance one day!

For the purpose of the following exercises we will be using the A string exclusively. The A string is the second string from the right when the violin is on your shoulder.

I CHOOSE A CHALLENGE

Listening is Learning!

One of the best ways to learn how to play and count fiddle music is to listen to a lot of it! There are so many styles in Canada alone that you will definitely find tunes and styles that you love. Music is everywhere—find a traditional radio station, take out some CDs from the library or start scouring YouTube for some great fiddle music. Also, ask your parents if there are any bands coming to your town with a fiddle player. After all…listening is learning!

Reel Patterns on the A String

The Time Signature

Let's start with a basic *reel* pattern. The time signature for a reel is 4/4:

The number on top (**4**) tells you that there are four beats in every bar (1 – 2 – 3 – 4), while the number below (**4**) tells you that the quarter note (♩) gets one beat.

A bar is a section of music defined by vertical bar lines. For example, there are two bars of music below. In each bar:

There are four *beats;*
The quarter note gets one beat.

1. *Get Set Up:* Remember all the important things you've learned so far about how to hold the bow and the violin—go through the *Bow Hold* and *Left Hand* checklists on pages 13 and 16, so you are remembering your good habits:

   ✦ Check your bow hold (all fingers rounded, including your thumb);

✦ Make sure your violin is sitting comfortably between your chin and shoulder;

✦ Even though you are not using your left hand for these exercises, this is a good time to begin checking that the left hand is set up properly—thumb across from index finger, straight left wrist and so on.

2. As you play the following patterns, try to stay in the *middle* part of the bow. You can ask your teacher to mark the middle of your bow with tape, as in the picture below.

3. When you move the bow on the string, try to imagine that your upper arm (your arm from your elbow to your shoulder) is flat against a wall so that it cannot move. As you play each note, the movement in your bow arm should start from *your elbow,* and not your shoulder.

4. Where is your bow on the string? The place where you will get the loudest and clearest *tone* (quality of sound) is called the "Kreisler Highway." It was named for the renowned violinist, Fritz Kreisler, who played with his bow on this section of string most of the time. Kreisler is still remembered for the clarity and sweetness of his tone. This spot, as you can see in the picture to the right, is about the same width as the hairs of your bow away from the bridge. You may have to keep your eyes on your bow or use a mirror to make sure that it stays there while you are playing!

5. Keep your *right arm loose and relaxed.* You will know that you are doing this when you see a little bit of movement in your right wrist. Once you are comfortable with the rhythms, you can use a mirror to observe your wrist and overall posture and set up.

6. I have included a spoken component under each exercise, so that rather than being tied to the music, you can easily remember the pattern and have your focus on the bow instead. You do not need to speak the pattern out loud—in your head is just fine!

7. Fiddle music is dance music. I have included *accents* (>), or *emphasized* notes in the following exercises so that you can discover the dance groove for each pattern. Whenever you see an accented note, use a bit more pressure on the bow by pressing down on your (right) index finger to give the bow more weight.

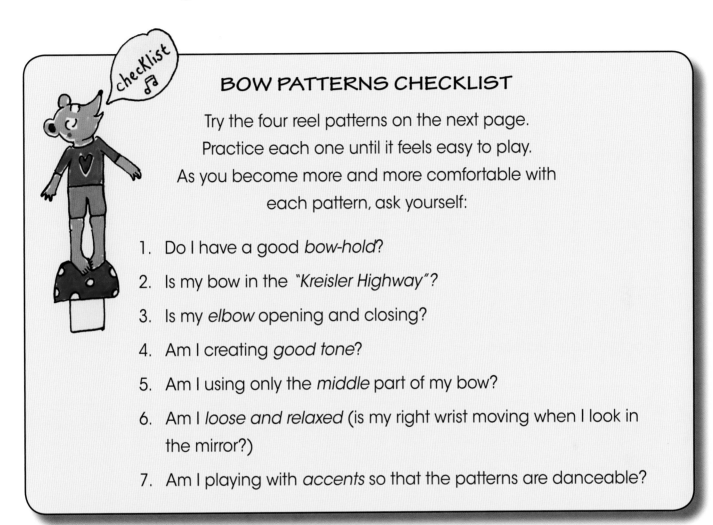

BOW PATTERNS CHECKLIST

Try the four reel patterns on the next page.
Practice each one until it feels easy to play.
As you become more and more comfortable with
each pattern, ask yourself:

1. Do I have a good *bow-hold*?

2. Is my bow in the *"Kreisler Highway"*?

3. Is my *elbow* opening and closing?

4. Am I creating *good tone*?

5. Am I using only the *middle* part of my bow?

6. Am I *loose and relaxed* (is my right wrist moving when I look in the mirror?)

7. Am I playing with *accents* so that the patterns are danceable?

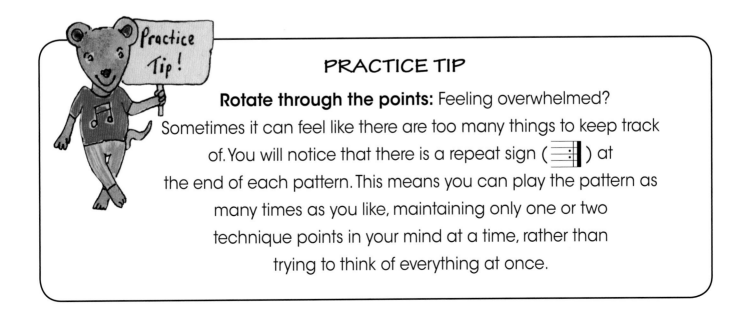

PRACTICE TIP

Rotate through the points: Feeling overwhelmed?
Sometimes it can feel like there are too many things to keep track
of. You will notice that there is a repeat sign ( ) at
the end of each pattern. This means you can play the pattern as
many times as you like, maintaining only one or two
technique points in your mind at a time, rather than
trying to think of everything at once.

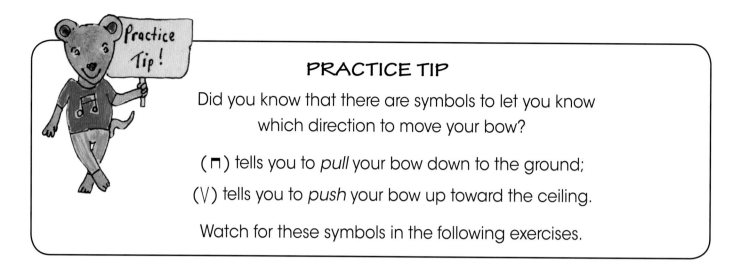

PRACTICE TIP

Did you know that there are symbols to let you know
which direction to move your bow?

(⊓) tells you to *pull* your bow down to the ground;

(∨) tells you to *push* your bow up toward the ceiling.

Watch for these symbols in the following exercises.

Basic Rhythm in 4/4

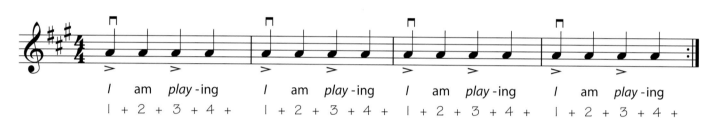

Run Doggy Reel Pattern

I'm a Little Monkey Reel Pattern

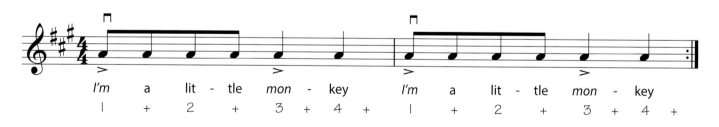

Huckleberry Huckleberry Reel Pattern

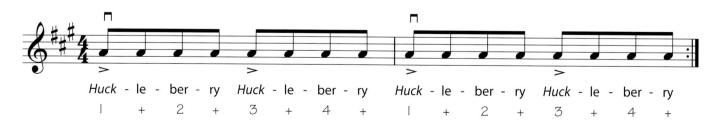

Waltz Patterns on the A String

The next type of rhythm that we're going to learn about is the *waltz* rhythm. The time signature for a waltz is 3/4:

The number on top (**3**) tells you that there are three beats in every bar (*1 – 2 – 3, 1 – 2 – 3*), while the number below (**4**) tells you that the quarter note (♩) gets one beat.

In a waltz pattern, the emphasis is on the first beat of each bar (i.e., *one – two – three, one – two – three*). Let's apply this:

Simple Waltz Pattern

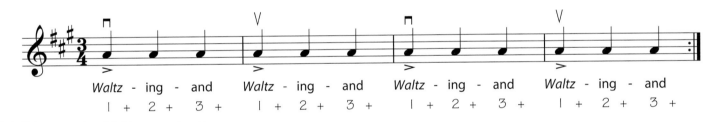

Another Waltz Pattern

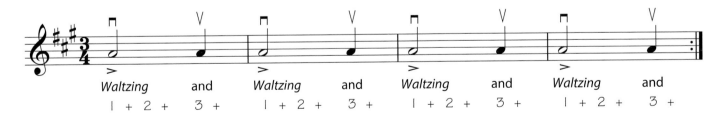

Jig Patterns on the A String

The final type of rhythm that we're going to cover is the *jig* rhythm. The time signature for a jig is 6/8:

The number on top (**6**) tells you that there are six beats in every bar (*1–2–3–4–5–6, 1–2–3–4–5–6*), while the number below (**8**) tells you that the eighth note (♪) gets one beat.

In a jig pattern, the emphasis is on the first and fourth beat of each bar (i.e., *one* – two – three – *four* – five – six; *one* – two – three – *four* – five – six).

Let's apply this.

Jig-gi-ty Jig-gi-ty Jig Pattern

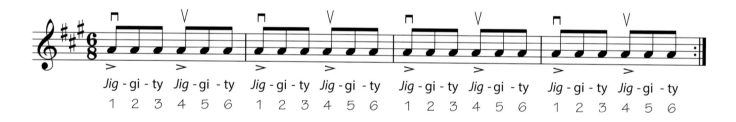

Down Jig-gi-ty Jig Pattern

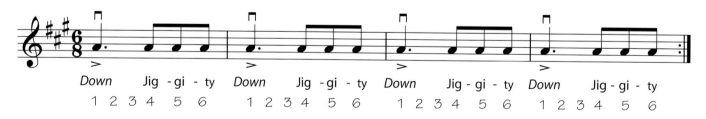

Yellow Bicycle Jig Pattern

Jig-gi-ty Up-Up Jig Pattern

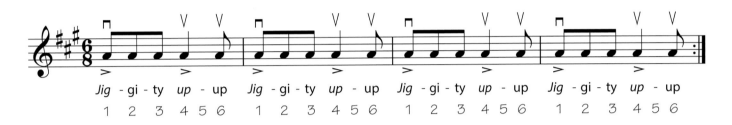

Once you are comfortable with the Waltz, Reel and Jig bow patterns, go back to the *Bow Patterns Checklist* on page 23 and see if you are incorporating each of the technique points mentioned.

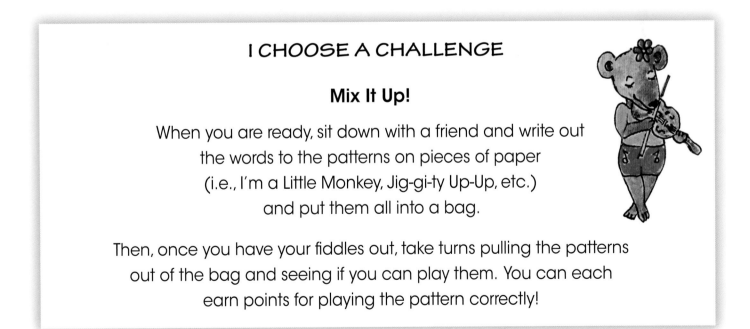

I CHOOSE A CHALLENGE

Mix It Up!

When you are ready, sit down with a friend and write out the words to the patterns on pieces of paper (i.e., I'm a Little Monkey, Jig-gi-ty Up-Up, etc.) and put them all into a bag.

Then, once you have your fiddles out, take turns pulling the patterns out of the bag and seeing if you can play them. You can each earn points for playing the pattern correctly!

PRACTICE TIP

Get a visual: Use a mirror in order to keep an eye on
your bow. Sometimes the bow is like a child at the supermarket—
as soon as you take your eyes off of it, it wanders away!

The best way to do this is to stand with the scroll of your violin pointing
at the mirror and then to turn your entire body 90 degrees to the left
so that your profile is reflected in the mirror. Now, turn only your
head towards the mirror without moving the rest of your body.
You should now have a good view of the bow position relative
to the bridge, as well as your entire right arm!

From this position you should be able to tell whether you have a good bow-hold,
whether your bow is on the Kreisler Highway, whether you are moving your right
arm from the elbow (and not the shoulder), and
whether you are playing in the middle of your bow.

Time to Pluck and Bow!

Time To Pluck and Bow!

Now that you have your left and right arm set up comfortably, it's time to introduce the fingers of your left hand to their places in the A Major Scale! Before you continue, you might want to review the *Violin Hold Checklist* and *Left Hand Checklist* on pages 16 and 18 to make sure that your violin and left hand are set up correctly.

In order to pluck the notes with good technique, you'll want to anchor your right hand to the fingerboard so that your right index finger stays close to the string that you want to pluck. Start by making a backwards "C" shape with the thumb and index finger of your right hand. Anchor the pad of your right thumb just under the top corner of the fingerboard (the end closest to the right sound hole), and curve your pointer finger over the strings. To pluck, pull gently on the string with the pad of your index finger.

On the next page, start with *Step 1*, and work your way up the scale to finish at *Step 8*. Above each note, you will see the name of that note (for example, the first note is A), and below each note is the string and finger you need to use to be able to play that note.

For example, for the first note, which is A, you will pluck the A string and not place any fingers on the fingerboard. The next note, B, is also played on the A string and you need to put your first finger down in order to pluck the B note, and so on.

Note that fingers 2 and 3 are close together for both the A and D scales, as shown in the picture below.

A Major Scale Orientation

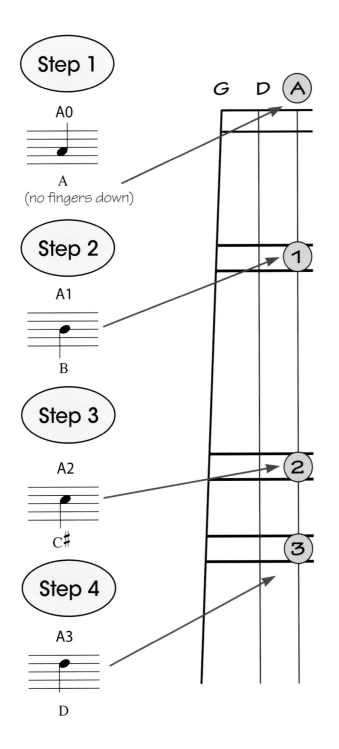

Step 1

A0

A

(no fingers down)

Step 2

A1

B

Step 3

A2

C#

Step 4

A3

D

Step 1

Fingers curved over the A string, left wrist straight, relaxed hand.

Step 2

Place 1st finger on the A string on the fingertip.

Step 3

Keeping 1st finger down, place 2nd finger on the A string on the fingertip.

Step 4

Keeping 1st and 2nd fingers down, place 3rd finger on the A string on the fingertip.

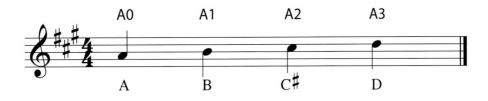

A0   A1   A2   A3

A   B   C#   D

Fingers curved over the
E string, left wrist straight,
relaxed hand.

E

Step 5

E0

E

(no fingers down)

Place 1st finger on the
E string on the fingertip.

1

Step 6

E1

F♯

Step 7

Keeping 1st finger down,
place 2nd finger on the
E string on the fingertip.

2

3

Step 7

E2

G♯

Keeping 1st and 2nd fingers
down, place 3rd finger on
the E string on the
fingertip.

Step 8

E3

A

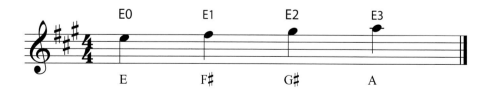

Look Mom! No Music!

For this Challenge, after you've plucked the notes from
Step 1 to Step 8 a few times, see if you can do the same
thing without looking at the diagram—can you play
all 8 notes from memory?

Most fiddlers play many tunes from memory, (some can play
hundreds of tunes from memory!) so it's a great idea
to start developing your music memory now!

Congratulations! Why am I congratulating you, you might ask? Because you just played your first scale—the *A major scale!* This one little scale is the building block to hundreds of fiddle tunes! On the next page, you will see what this scale looks like when it is written in the musical staff. First though, let's just take a moment to talk about an important part of the musical staff—the *key signature*.

The Key Signature

Two important components of the musical staff are the *time signature*, which we discussed on page 21, and the *key signature*, shown below.

The key signature for the key of A Major is made up of three *sharps*, represented by the ♯ symbol. In music, the word sharp means "higher in pitch by a semitone" (or *half-step*). The three sharps in the key of A Major are F♯, C♯ and G♯. Have a second look at the *A Major Scale Orientation* on pages 31 and 32, noticing where each of those sharps are located in the scale along with their corresponding finger positions. The left hand finger placement for each of the following plucked A Major Scale exercises will be exactly as you see in the diagram.

For all of the following exercises, once you have plucked the scale a few times and feel comfortable with your left hand finger placement, try playing the scale using your bow.

A Major Scale: Whole Notes

A *whole note* looks like a round donut, and is held for *four* counts:

A Major Scale: Quarter Notes

The next scale is still the A Major scale, but it looks different. That's because it's written in *quarter notes*. A quarter note is held for one count. Play each note of the following scale four times, and hold each note for one count. Give it a try!

PRACTICE TIP

A very important component of practice is taking the time to separate right and left hand use. That's why Section 3 took you through the basic rhythms on open strings, emphasizing *right arm* practice, before introducing the left hand to the notes of the A Major scale in Section 4.

As you play through these next exercises and become familiar with the notes, see if you can separate your practice time into the following three components:

1. Focus on the *right arm*, paying attention to bow hold and those items on your Bow Hold and Bow Patterns checklist on pages 13 and 23. For this segment of your practice, don't worry so much about what your left hand is doing;

2. Focus on the *left arm*, paying attention to those items on the Left Hand checklist on page 18. For this segment of your practice, either pluck the notes, or use the bow, but don't worry so much about what your right arm is doing;

3. Once you have warmed up with both right and left side checklists, try *putting it all together!*

I'm A Little Monkey Reel Pattern: Climbing the A string!

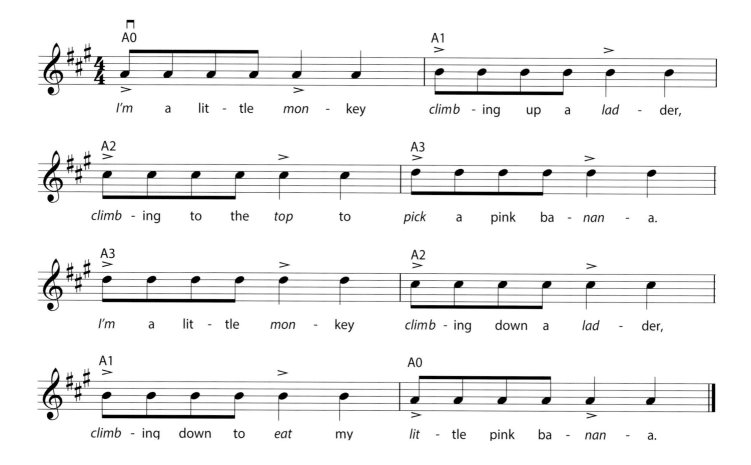

I'm A Little Monkey Reel Pattern: Climbing the E string!

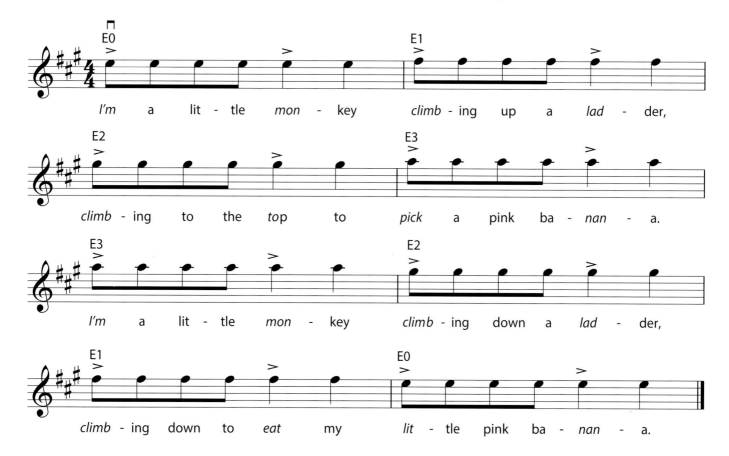

I CHOOSE A CHALLENGE

I Know My Notes on the A and E strings!

For this Challenge, after you've plucked the A Major scale
and named all the notes as you plucked them, see if you can
name the notes without looking at the music. You can also pluck
the notes and have a friend name them as you go, and then switch!
Since you're playing in the key of A Major, don't forget to say "sharp"
when you name the F♯, C♯ and G♯ notes in the scale.

Simple Waltz Pattern

Another Waltz Pattern

Run Doggy Reel Pattern

Huckleberry Huckleberry Reel Pattern

Jig-gi-ty Jig-gi-ty Jig Pattern

Down Jig-gi-ty Jig Pattern

Yellow Bicycle Jig Pattern

Jig-gi-ty Up-Up Jig Pattern

Once you have plucked and bowed through the A Major scale patterns, continue to refine your technique skills by incorporating checklist points as you go. Remember to focus on only *one* point at a time, and cycle through the points so that your technique becomes automatic over time.

D Major Scale Orientation

Step 1

D0

D

(no fingers down)

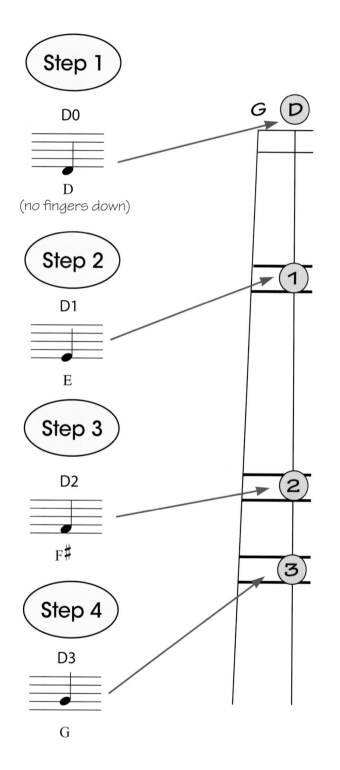

Step 2

D1

E

Step 3

D2

F♯

Step 4

D3

G

Step 1

Fingers curved over the D string, left wrist straight, relaxed hand.

Step 2

Place 1st finger on the D string on the fingertip.

Step 3

Keeping 1st finger down, place 2nd finger on the D string on the fingertip.

Step 4

Keeping 1st and 2nd fingers down, place 3rd finger on the D string on the fingertip.

Step 5

Fingers curved over the A string, left wrist straight, relaxed hand.

Step 6

Place 1st finger on the A string on the fingertip.

Step 7

Keeping 1st finger down, place 2nd finger on the A string on the fingertip.

Step 8

Keeping 1st and 2nd fingers down, place 3rd finger on the A string on the fingertip.

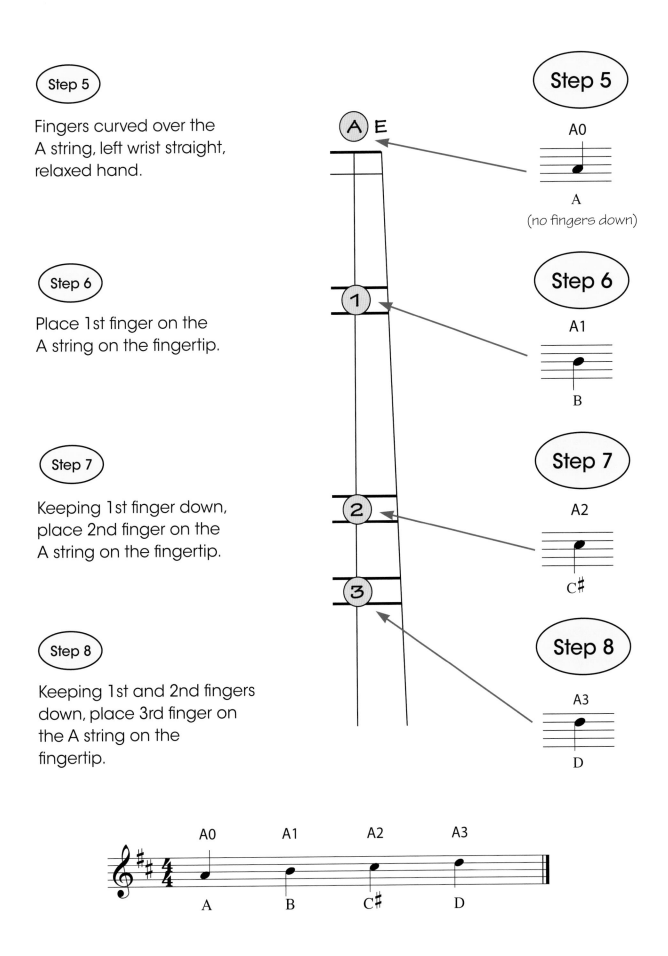

The Key Signature

The key signature for the key of D Major is made up of two sharps: F♯ and C♯. Have a second look at the *D Major Scale Orientation* on pages 42 and 43, noticing where each of those sharps are located in the scale along with their corresponding finger positions.

The left hand finger placement for each of the following plucked D Major Scale exercises will be exactly as you see in the diagram on pages 42 and 43.

D Major Scale: Whole Notes

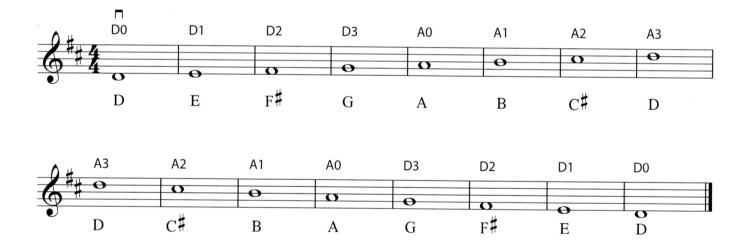

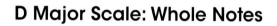

D Major Scale — Quarter Notes

I'm a Little Monkey — Climbing the D string!

Simple Waltz Pattern

Another Waltz Pattern

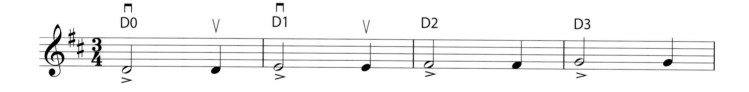

Run Doggy Reel Pattern

Huckleberry Huckleberry Reel Pattern

Jig-gi-ty Jig-gi-ty Jig Pattern

Down Jig-gi-ty Jig Pattern

Yellow Bicycle Jig Pattern

Jig-gi-ty Up-Up

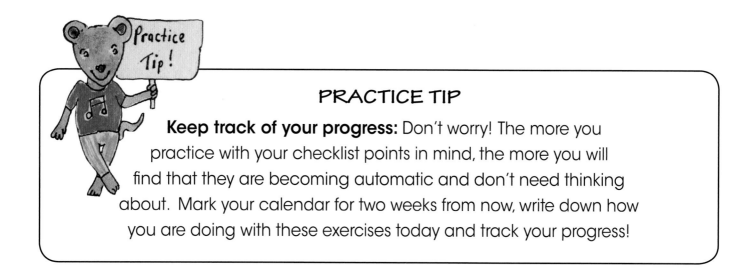
My First Tune on Three Strings

Hot Cross Buns: Fun on the A String!

Hot Cross Buns: Fun on the E String!

Hot Cross Buns: Fun on the D String!

Checklists and More!

 # Checklists

BOW HOLD CHECKLIST

1. Curly: Is the pointer finger curled over the grip?

2. Are the *Two Best Friends* (middle fingers) sticking together, just like best friends, and dangling their feet over the bridge?

3. Is the *King of the Castle* (pinky) nice and round and resting on the top of the stick of the bow?

4. Is *Knuckles the Thumb* also nice and round, leaning against the "bump" of the frog?

VIOLIN HOLD CHECKLIST

1. Check to make sure your *body is loose* and relaxed, and that your hips and knees are not locked;

2. Where are you *looking?* If you are looking up at the ceiling or down at the ground, adjust your shoulder rest so that you are looking straight across the room;

3. Your *left foot* should be slightly forward and to the left so that your weight is evenly balanced over both feet;

4. Your spine and neck should follow in a *straight line* — your chin rest is for resting your chin and part of your jaw, but not your cheek;

5. Your nose, left foot and scroll should all point in the same direction.

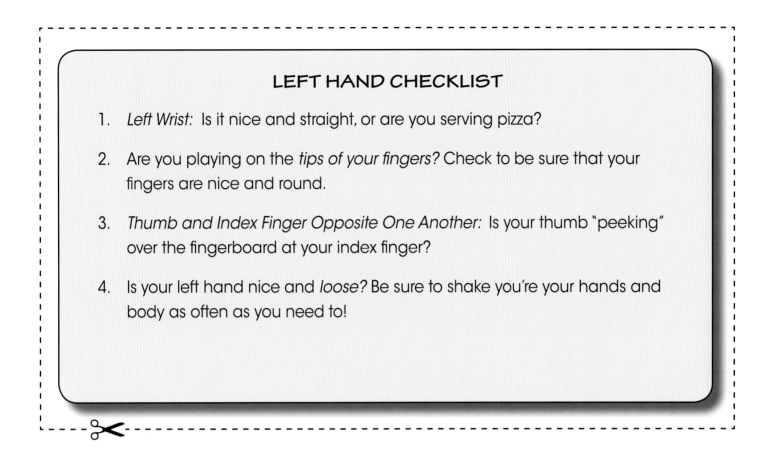

LEFT HAND CHECKLIST

1. *Left Wrist:* Is it nice and straight, or are you serving pizza?

2. Are you playing on the *tips of your fingers?* Check to be sure that your fingers are nice and round.

3. *Thumb and Index Finger Opposite One Another:* Is your thumb "peeking" over the fingerboard at your index finger?

4. Is your left hand nice and *loose?* Be sure to shake you're your hands and body as often as you need to!

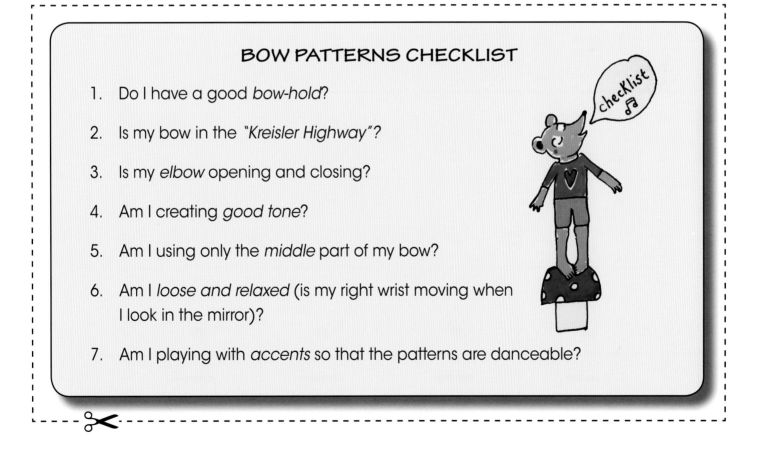

BOW PATTERNS CHECKLIST

1. Do I have a good *bow-hold*?

2. Is my bow in the *"Kreisler Highway"*?

3. Is my *elbow* opening and closing?

4. Am I creating *good tone*?

5. Am I using only the *middle* part of my bow?

6. Am I *loose and relaxed* (is my right wrist moving when I look in the mirror)?

7. Am I playing with *accents* so that the patterns are danceable?

 # Note Values

Note	Name	Beats
𝅝	Whole Note	4 Beats
𝅗𝅥	Half Note	2 Beats
𝅘𝅥	Quarter Note	1 Beat
𝅘𝅥𝅮 or 𝅘𝅥𝅮𝅘𝅥𝅮	Eighth Note	1/2 Beat

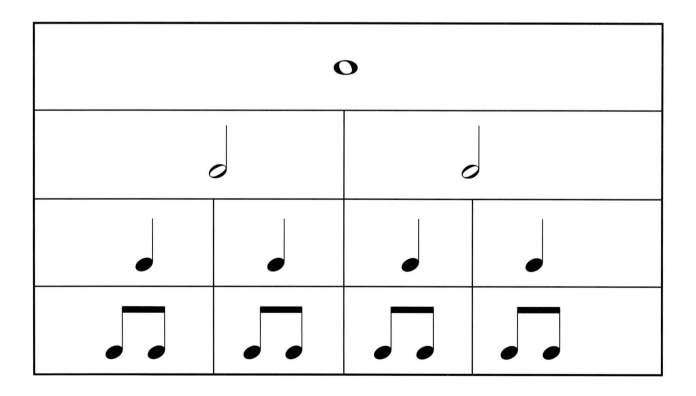

Time and Key Signatures

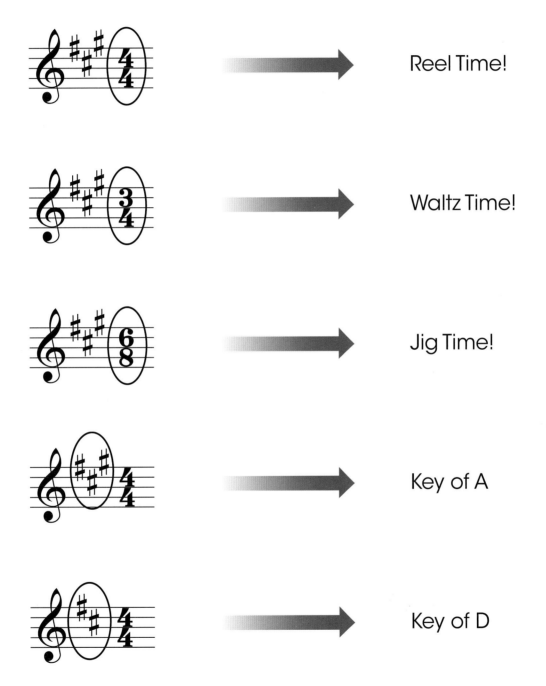

Reel Time!

Waltz Time!

Jig Time!

Key of A

Key of D

Also in this series:

Once Upon a String
Volume 1

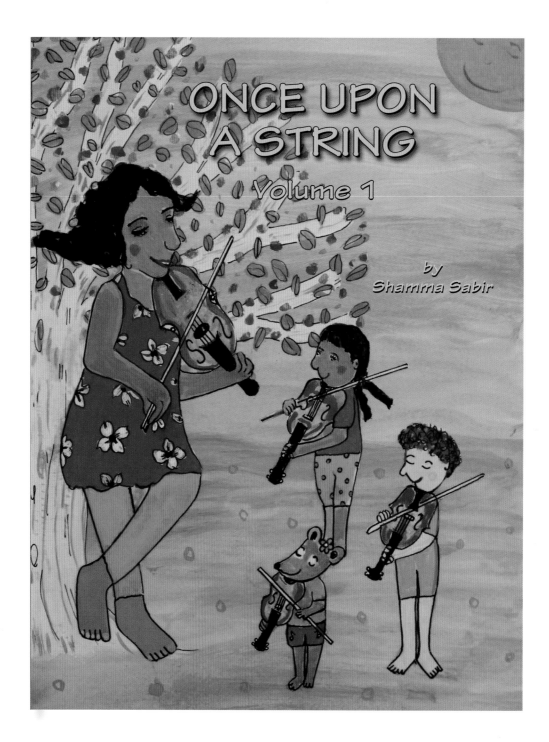